HOW I EARNED OVER $1 MILLION USING NONE OF MY OWN MONEY

HOW I EARNED OVER $1 MILLION USING NONE OF MY OWN MONEY

8 LESSONS I LEARNED FROM MY FIRST REAL ESTATE DEAL

Andrea Pryce

ISBN: 1530618746
ISBN 13: 9781530618743

Preface

This book was written for those who want to get started on their journey toward making their first $1 million, those who are looking for a steady and reliable flow of passive income but who do not have the funds to get started, those who are looking to start investing in income-producing real estate properties but are on the fence about how to get started, those who are currently investing in real estate but their returns are less than stellar, and those who think investing in commercial real estate is out of their reach.

I wrote this book to tell the story of my actual experiences with closing on my first multiple-unit commercial property with no personal money down and no initial real estate experience. It discusses my trials, errors, and triumphs and summarizes the eight lessons I learned by successfully closing on and managing a property that enabled me to earn over $1 million during my tenure of ownership.

This book shows how I started my journey of real estate investing without knowing anything concrete about real estate. I did not let my inexperience of the subject of real estate investing and my errors along the way stop me from accomplishing my goal of owning an income-producing property. I learned along the way and kept going despite setbacks, which ultimately led to my success. I hope my story will be an inspiration to you to get started on your own real estate investment journey. Enjoy!

INTRODUCTION

I made well over a million dollars from my first real estate investment without spending a penny from my own pocket. I bought a multifamily residential building for $224,000, sold it years later for triple the purchase price, and collected over $800,000 in rental income during my time of ownership.

Just about now, you are probably saying, "*Right.* Is that even possible? You spent none of your money, and you made over a million dollars?" The answer is yes! It is very possible— I did it!

Buying real estate costs money. However, it doesn't have to be *your* money. With the right mix of resourcefulness, creativity, and knowledge, you can buy real estate with no money of your own. I speak from experience. I did it by dispelling all the myths naysayers tell you about real estate investments.

I know that financing your first investment property can be daunting. But as they say, it's usually the things we don't do that we regret later in life. So, if concerns about financing your first property are stopping you from getting started, my story can serve as motivation for you. I learned a lot of valuable lessons along the way. Some lessons I learned the hard way, and some were easy. I would like to pass these valuable lessons on to you so that you can go the easy route. Here is my story.

MY STORY

I had $18,000 in savings, and I knew I wanted to do something productive with this money. I was planning on purchasing a home and using the $18,000 as a down payment.

Around this same time, a friend introduced me to two books that changed my life forever: *Think and Grow Rich*, by Napoleon Hill, and *Cashflow Quadrant*, by Robert Kiyosaki. The concepts of these books were simple, yet mind-blowing for me. My whole point of view on life changed. The ideas put forth in these books became the driving force for the way I lived my life and the actions I took from then on. I was especially taken by one of Hill's simple quotes—"Whatever the mind can conceive and believe, it can achieve"—and Kiyosaki's idea that a house is a liability and that your money should be working for you instead of you working for your money. These books changed how I looked at money, assets, and liabilities.

I quickly turned my attention to my personal finances and knew that I needed to focus on generating passive income—that is, income received on a regular basis, with little effort required to maintain it. During this time, I also started learning about real estate investing, and there seemed to be a lot of positives to it. Real estate investing seemed to be more stable than the stock market for wealth building and had several additional benefits as well. I started to rethink what I wanted to do with my money. I wanted this money to go to work for me. So I scrapped the idea of buying a home. Instead, I decided to buy an income-generating investment property. Once I made up my mind, there was no turning back.

LESSON 1

KNOW SPECIFICALLY WHAT YOU WANT

Now that I had decided to buy an investment income property, the question became, where do I begin? I have always heard the best deals in real estate are foreclosure properties, but the insiders always had access to these properties long before they were released to the general public. By the time this information got to the public, the best deals were already gone. To be a part of the insiders, you had to pay for it.

So, given my belief, I immediately subscribed to a weekly foreclosure listing. The subscription required that I pay in advance for the listing, and the company would send me an updated weekly listing with the latest foreclosed homes and bank-owned properties for sale. In theory, subscribers would get access to this weekly listing of the latest properties available for sale before the general public would—*in theory.*

When the first listing arrived, I was so excited. It had well over a hundred properties of various types. Since I had no idea what type of property I was specifically looking to buy, I was glad there were so many different types of properties in this listing. I started my search with a sense of assurance. However, after about four weeks of using these listings, going all over the city, and looking at all types of real estate properties, I realized that it was a waste of my time. The information in these listings was too varied and most of the time outdated.

Furthermore, I figured out that there were so many free real estate listings online, paying for any listing was unnecessary. What I needed was to know exactly what I wanted. What *did* I want? After figuring this out, I quickly cancelled my subscription and decided to use the free online listings.

I reevaluated my goals and made them more precise. I narrowed my focus to a specific type of real estate—namely, multifamily properties.

I decided to purchase a multifamily residential building with six or more units and to do so within the next two months. In addition, I wanted to get it at such a bargain price that in the event that half of the tenant population did not pay their rents on any given month, the mortgage would still be covered.

Knowing what you want is extremely important. However, it is a step that is often overlooked by most people—including me—because we do not perceive it as being an important step. Knowing what you want can save you a lot of time, money, and effort. Because I did not at first have a clear sense of what type of property I wanted to buy, I started my search with unclear and confusing information and spent money unnecessarily on such information. Once I decided the type of investment property I was interested in buying, I was able to narrow my focus and stay motivated. My search became easier because I was able to narrow down my search using free real estate websites.

Lesson Learned: *Knowing exactly what you want will save you time and money, so approach every deal knowing exactly what you want.*

LESSON 2

BUY THE STORY, NOT THE SOURCE

I knew that if I wanted to accomplish my new goal of purchasing a multifamily residential building with six or more units at a bargain price, I would have to look not only at the property, but also at the owner's story. What was the real reason for the sale?

I needed to do background research and evaluate multiple properties before making offers so as to make a smart financial decision. From that point on, every evening after work, instead of turning on the television and vegging out, I dedicated at least two hours to the pursuit of finding a property through searches on free sites such as century21.com and others. On the weekends, a contractor friend and I would go out and look at the properties I had found online. We checked out several properties within my price range, including properties I didn't like, so that I could assess the different neighborhoods and have a better sense of my target property's value.

The first thing I did when I started looking for a property was to look for an area in the city I thought would have possibilities, both quality-wise and price-wise. Once I found a location that interested me, I proceeded to find all I could about the area itself, beyond the immediate block on which the property was located. I did all this before talking to the owners.

When I found properties that fit my criteria, I talked with the owners or the property managers and learned their stories and their reasons for selling. I usually begin the conversation with the seller by talking about him or her. What was the reason for selling? How long had he or she lived on the property, if at all? I asked any questions I could think of that related to the seller, the motivation for selling, and what the seller was looking for. Some were guarded, while others opened up easily with their reasons for selling. In the process, I learned a lot about the motivation and intentions of the sellers. After a few weeks of doing this, I found the right property, accompanied by the right story. I was *sold*!

It was a six-family building located in a lower-income neighborhood. The current owner had twenty properties, including this particular property, around the New York City area. He was in the process of selling them all because he was retiring and moving back to his home country. He had already sold seventeen of them, and this building was among the last of the remaining three properties. He was more than ready to get this chapter of his life closed and was eager to start the next one, but he was not getting any interested buyers for this particular building. The main reason for the lack of interest was that this building was in a low-income area (a.k.a. the ghetto). In addition to location, the rent roll was very low, two of the six tenants were not paying their rents, and the apartments needed some updating. There was my story!

The property was listed at $300,000, which was priced slightly below market to sell. I made an offer of $200,000 because I knew his story. The real estate agent who was handling the sale initially refused to take my offer to the seller because he believed it was too low and would be a waste of his time. The agent stated that the seller would not entertain any offers below $250,000. I reminded him that by law, all offers must be presented to the seller. So my first offer of $200,000 was presented to the seller. After some back and forth with a few counteroffers, we settled on the purchase price of $212,000.

I was able to negotiate the best possible deal with this seller because I knew his story and that he was motivated to sell this property. Buying the story allowed me to enter into a very favorable contract with plenty of built-in equity. In addition to this one, there are many other factors that will motivate someone to sell, such as retiring, health-related issues, an out-of-state owner, an owner's job transfer, a death in the family, foreclosure, or divorce. Yes, you need to look for the right seller with the right story that fits you and your goals.

Once we agreed on the purchase price, I signed the purchase contract for closing within forty-five days, pending a mortgage. With that settled, I set out to find a mortgage.

Lesson Learned: *Taking the time to learn the seller's story enabled me to negotiate the best possible purchase price with confidence because I was able to buy the story and not the building.*

LESSON 3

You Don't Have to Have Money to Start Investing in Real Estate

I had always heard and believed that you have to have money to start investing in real estate. So from the moment I decided to purchase an investment property, I started an aggressive savings plan. By the time I found this six-family building, I had a total of $30,000 (my initial $18,000 and $12,000 from my aggressive saving). I was so proud of myself. I had enough money for the down payment and closing costs—or so I thought. I was ready to move forward with my purchase.

First things first: find a mortgage. To my surprise, I learned that multifamily residential buildings with six or more units are considered commercial properties. As such, a typical commercial mortgage requires a minimum 30 percent down payment. This meant in order to purchase this property, I would have to come to the table with $75,600, which comprised the down payment of $63,600 (30 percent of the purchase price) plus $12,000 of estimated closing costs.

At this point, I quickly realized that my $30,000 was not nearly enough. I needed an additional $45,600 to close on this deal. Where was I going to get the money?

Knowing my dilemma, my contractor friend—the one who was by my side throughout this whole process—came to me with a win-win proposal. I needed to raise an additional $45,600 in the next forty-five days. His sister needed a short-term loan, repayable within a few days, and she was willing to pay a high rate of interest for this loan. He proposed that we help each other out, allowing everyone to win. His sister would get the help she needed, and the interest she paid in return for my help would be a good start for me toward raising that additional $45,600.

His sister, who had a high-end retail clothing business, was having trouble clearing some inventory coming in from France as it was stuck on the shipping dock. She needed an additional $70,000 to cover the inventory cost, and he, my contractor friend, had only $40,000 to loan her. She was looking for an emergency bridge loan and would return the money within three days at 15 percent interest, which meant $4,500 in interest income for me. My friend assured me that my money would be safe. In addition, I had some knowledge about his sister's business. She had a good niche business going, and she was a well-respected person within the community. I willingly offered up my $30,000. I joyfully told myself that this was going to be the easiest $4,500 I had ever made. Now with this substantial interest income, I would only need to find $29,100 plus the estimated closing costs. Things were looking up!

I think you know where this story is going. Three days later, *no money.* One week later, *no money!* We had been scammed! It turns out that his sister secretly had a gambling problem and was spending the revenue from her business to support her extreme gambling habits instead of paying business expenses. She was at the point where her creditors were seizing her assets, including the inventory shipment that was sitting on the dock. That is why the inventory was sitting on the dock and not in the stores. After learning the truth, we were not able to recover any of the money. She had gambled *all* the money away within days of receiving it. As a matter of fact, we learned that the very same day she had received the money from us, she went directly to the Atlantic City casinos to gamble. Needless to say, my contractor friend felt embarrassed and ashamed by the actions of his sister.

Words could not describe the way I felt. I was devastated! I was literally sick to my stomach. This touched the core of my being in a very bad way. I was wallowing in self-pity. However, after a few days of self-pity, I knew I had to end it. I regrouped and decided to move forward.

Now with no money and a scheduled closing in less than forty-five days, I needed a miracle in order to call this building my own. I was not going to give up on getting this property. No was not an option.

That night, I went to bed with my head spinning, trying to think of every possible way of getting the required money to close this deal. While I was sleeping, my mind went to work. I woke up the next morning refreshed and with a three-step plan.

Step 1: Ask the seller to pay the closing costs. Since the seller was more than ready to start the next chapter of his life, I had no problem asking him to pay the estimated $12,000 closing costs. He agreed to pay them through what's called a seller's concession. A seller's concession is an amount that a seller agrees to contribute to the buyer toward the closing costs. This contribution is then financed over the life of the loan within the purchase price. So the new purchase price was now $224,000.

Step 2: Ask the bank for a concession on the 30 percent down payment requirement. The bank appraiser valued this property for more than the seller's asking price; therefore, this property had more than enough built-in equity to start with. With this information, I had no problem asking the bank for a concession on the 30 percent down payment requirement. With some negotiations, we ended up agreeing to a 25 percent down payment. I had an approved mortgage for 75 percent of the new purchase price of $224,000. Now, I needed only $56,000 (25 percent of the new purchase price). With this behind me, I felt like I was on top of the world. Keep in mind that, at this point, I still didn't have any money, but I was feeling very hopeful.

Step 3: Get a personal loan for as much as possible from the bank. A personal loan is an unsecured loan from the bank that is granted for personal use. The loan is based on the borrower's established consumer credit and ability to pay. Banks look at past credit history, so I was able to approach more than one bank to request multiple loans. Since the mortgage for the six-family building was a commercial mortgage, it would not show on my credit because it was based on the financials of the building itself. I was granted two personal loans from two different banks totaling $50,000. Now, things were really looking up. At this point, I was less than twenty days away from closing, and I felt very relieved. I only had a $6,000 shortfall, and I knew that at closing, there would be enough credits (proration of rent collected, tenants' security deposits, and so forth) to cover the shortfall.

I went to the closing with confidence. The closing went well, and when the dust settled, I walked out with ownership of a building and a check for $5,600. Now I was the proud owner of a six-family building, and I had not used a penny of my own money to purchase this building.

Buying real estate with nothing out of your own pocket is very possible. Money is still required, but other people's money is used rather than your own. There are many creative ways to finance real estate, and they are completely legal and sometimes very ingenious. It took losing my money to learn that I did not have to spend a penny of my own money to start investing in real estate. I never got back my money, but the lesson I learned was invaluable. I learned this lesson the hard way, but I am happy I learned it.

Lesson Learned: *You truly do not have to have money to get started in real estate investing. With the will to get started and some creativity, other people's money is there just waiting for you to use it.*

LESSON 4

FINANCING FUTURE VENTURES GETS EASIER

N ow you might be saying to yourself, that's a lot of loans to repay. Yes, I had three loans on which to make monthly payments, but I was not sweating it. The monthly income that the building was generating at the time of closing was more than enough to make these payments comfortably. Furthermore, since I had bought the building with built-in equity, within a short period of time I was able to refinance the property at a lower interest rate, repay the two personal loans, and attain money for renovations, all while lowering my monthly mortgage payment.

Furthermore, as my property appreciated, I was able to leverage the equity from this building to help finance other investment rental properties and the purchase of an established retail business.

Having my first property made it easier to obtain mortgages with great rates in order to finance future projects. With the use of investment mortgages, I was able to increase my investment power. This helped me maximize the investment returns through leveraging. Leveraging is using other people's money for investments so that you use less of your own money. By using other people's money, I was able to buy more properties and increase my returns with minimal cash of my own invested.

Lesson Learned: *Just like a baby taking her first step, the first one is always the hardest. Once the first deal is completed successfully, financing other deals thereafter is much easier.*

LESSON 5

PEOPLE ARE ALL THE SAME

I had the building. Now what? Since it was located in a so-called low-income neighborhood, when I told people where I had bought my building, most freaked out, telling me to get out while I could. What a waste of money. You will never get your rent. Those people will destroy your place. Those tenants are going to be a headache. You are going to be a slumlord. The list of negative comments from the naysayers went on and on.

After hearing enough of these comments, doubt started to seep into my mind. I did not want to be a slumlord. I told myself I did not know how to relate to "ghetto" people. What in the world had I gotten myself into? Now, all kinds of fears built up in my mind about my tenants, and

I had not even met them yet. I just knew them based on what people were saying—"Those people are scary!"—and these naysayers didn't even know them, either. I bit the bullet and decided to meet with my tenants individually.

After the meetings, I realized my fears were unfounded. People are people. There are good and not so good people in every walk of life, and the good definitely outweigh the bad. I learned that we were all looking for the same things. My tenants, just like anyone else, wanted a nice and safe place to live and raise their families. They had the same basic priorities as everyone else: a home that was pleasing to the eye, convenient with relevant amenities, and structurally solid and safe. I learned that as long as these basic needs were met, most of the tenants were more than willing to pay their rent. Those who weren't paying would have to go. I came out of the meetings knowing exactly how to approach running this building.

Lesson Learned: *Get in the habit of judging people by the content of their character and not by their stations in life. In doing so, you can capitalize on opportunities that the average person would otherwise miss and later regret.*

LESSON 6

INCREASE TOTAL RENTAL INCOME BY RENOVATING AND ROTATING

Years later, when I was selling the building, a very popular question of prospective buyers was, "How is your rental income so high, yet the tenants are long-term?" During their property searches, these prospective buyers were seeing the opposite on comparable properties, regardless of the neighborhood. The answer was simple: renovation and rotation.

When I was in the process of purchasing the building, I saw that the apartments were in need of renovation, and, eventually, it had to get done. From meeting with each of my tenants individually, I knew that I wanted to keep four out of my six tenants.

I remembered reading somewhere that in order to avoid the actual eviction process, you can send a letter to the tenant simply *threatening* eviction, and the tenant will most likely leave. I did just that with the two tenants whom I wanted to leave. One took the bait and left immediately, and the other did not. I knew I had to deal with her at some point, but for now, I just wanted an empty apartment to get started on my plan: Operation Rent Increase.

I totally renovated the now-vacant apartment. When I was finished, this apartment looked nothing like any of the other apartments in the building. It looked modern, larger, bright, and very airy. In addition to the complete renovation, I outfitted the vacant apartment with new appliances. Renovation complete, the apartment looked like it belonged in an upscale neighborhood. Now, instead of bringing a new tenant into the building, I offered the newly renovated apartment to a handpicked existing tenant—at the higher market rent, of course.

Now this is where the psychology comes into play. Human beings always want to feel special and to be part of something, to be in the "in crowd." My selecting this specific tenant for the newly renovated apartment made him feel special, and he was more than willing to pay the higher rent. He felt like he was a part of something big. Even better, the other tenants now wanted to be selected for the next renovated apartment. I had to start a waiting list, and this enabled me to charge the highest possible market rent that the law allowed.

I repeated this process until all four of the tenants that I wanted to keep were rotated into newly renovated apartments at market rates. I then asked the tenants for a recommendation for the fifth apartment and ended up with a new, high-quality tenant.

With the five apartments bringing in higher rental income, I could now turn my attention to the tenant whom I did not want to keep. It turns out that my instinct was right. She was a so-called professional tenant. A professional tenant is one who moves into an apartment and pays the first few months' rent, but then makes no more payments;

once evicted, she starts the process all over again at another place.

When the previous owner was selling the building, he had posted the for-sale sign on the building. This lady used this as a perfect opportunity to become a resident of the building because she figured that the previous owner would not be as diligent with the background check since he was in the process of selling the building. She was right. So I inherited her with the building.

She was eventually evicted, and her apartment was renovated and rented out to a quality tenant recommended by one of my current tenants.

From this process, I learned that the best way to increase your rent roll is to start from within and then move out by renovating and rotating. I learned that a well-maintained rental property ensures not only happy tenants but also higher rents. There are many things you can do to increase your property's appeal to current and prospective tenants and increase the rental return in the process. Although it is difficult to put a figure on how much the improvements will increase your rental return, keeping your property well-maintained and up to date, makes it attractive to tenants. It makes good sense for you to spend money on your existing assets to increase the rental return because doing so creates more cash-flow. The renovations kept my maintenance costs down because ultimately, they attracted and kept tenants who took good care of their beautiful new apartments. Because of this, over the years, the renovations helped pay for themselves.

Lesson Learned: *Renovation and rotation have not only increased my rent roll but have also stabilized my building with happy tenants and, in the long-term, kept my cash flow steady.*

LESSON 7

MANAGE THE BUILDING FROM WITHIN

One of the biggest reasons people do not want to be landlords is that they believe tenants will call them at odd hours of the night for emergencies and repairs. This was one of my concerns from the beginning, so I took someone's advice and set up a 1-800 telephone line for the tenants to call with their concerns.

I quickly realized this was not for me because I still had to check the messages and then follow up on them. At the time, I was still working full-time at a demanding job and did not have the time or desire to hear about tenants' problems, repairs, or emergencies.

I looked into having a management company run the building. Management companies deal directly with prospects and tenants, saving you time and worry over marketing your rentals, collecting rent, handling maintenance and repair issues, responding to tenant complaints, and even pursuing evictions. Although hiring a property management company has many advantages, using one can be expensive.

I contacted some management companies, but because of the location of my property (the ghetto), the management companies wanted to charge me higher-than-normal management fees. I quickly dismissed that idea because I knew it was not the solution for this building. Then it hit me: Why don't I have one of the tenants manage the building? I remembered from my meetings with the tenants that one was a barber, and he had indicated he was saving to fulfill a lifelong dream of opening his own barbershop someday. This gave me a perfect idea on how I could help him fast-track his dream.

I approached him with a proposal to reduce his monthly rent by 40 percent, so he could have additional money to put toward his dream of owning a barbershop, in return for managing the building for me. He gladly accepted. This turned out to be one of the best decisions I have ever made.

He was so grateful that he now had a chance to put additional money toward saving for his dream of opening his very own barbershop that he did a phenomenal job as my on-site property manager. He went above and beyond the call of duty. He took all the tenants' calls. He kept the building and its surrounding areas pristine. He kept my common areas painted and looking fresh. He made all necessary repairs on the building and was always on hand to look after the property. He kept tabs on the outside security to ensure the building remained presentable (reporting people loitering, checking to make sure the gardens were kept up, etc.). He made sure tenants were keeping the common areas of the property clean. If a tenant had an issue with another tenant or a maintenance request, it was easy for him or her to contact someone in the same building who was available. When any prospective tenant wanted to see a unit, the manager was able to show the vacancy instantly, which increased my chances of filling the vacancy sooner. His proximity to the tenants was of great help to me. He was the first to notice if a tenant had breached a lease, abandoned a unit, or had an illegal pet, unregistered houseguest, or illegally parked vehicle. All he asked for in return was reimbursement for any supplies that he purchased from his own pocket, which I gladly gave.

When he moved on to open his own business, I replaced him with another tenant who was a plumber with the same offer of a 40 percent rental reduction. This plumber was an immigrant from the Caribbean, and his dream was to open a fast-food style Caribbean restaurant. Being my on-site property manager with the 40 percent rent reduction was a good opportunity to save toward his dream. The plumber eventually opened his Caribbean restaurant, and I replaced him with yet another tenant who was a construction worker. He too, did a phenomenal job, just like the others before him. When I was selling the building, all the prospective buyers commented on how the building was so well-kept. They could not believe that I did not have a management company running the place.

Lesson Learned: *Everybody has dreams, and by knowing my tenants' dreams and offering to help them accomplish their dreams, I created loyal tenants, which enabled me to manage the building efficiently and effectively from within.*

LESSON 8

LOW-INCOME NEIGHBORHOOD DOES NOT MEAN LOW RENT

Every time a so-called ghetto neighborhood is mentioned on TV, it is always in reference to the unemployed, underemployed, Section 8, or welfare recipients. If you listen to what is said on TV, you would think that the aforementioned types of people are the only people who live in these kinds of neighborhoods.

Of course, you now know from my firsthand experience that this is not true. There is also a diverse population of different professionals (teachers, plumbers, nurses, bus drivers, mechanics, bookkeepers, construction workers, and so on) who live in low-income neighborhoods for a variety of reasons. They just do not make the news. Some are new immigrants to the country; others grew up in the area and decided to stay; for some, it's the close proximity to work; some just don't realize they can pay the same rent in a so-called better neighborhood; and some just plain like the area. But whatever the reasons, you as a landlord, can attract high-quality tenants who are willing to pay the higher rent for living in your building as long as you provide a nice, clean and secure place to live.

I have found that some of the best tenants are immigrants. Most immigrants I have encountered have an intense drive to improve their situations; as they moved on, they always left my place better than they found it.

I found that attracting quality tenants with stable jobs to my building provided stability to the rental income stream and lowered the vacancy rate. The most important part is that you have to be willing to do your due diligence upfront and vet the tenants as best as possible. I recommend that you spare no expense in the vetting process, because it pays off in the end.

In general, low-income people aren't much more problematic than higher-income people, if you screen them properly up front. This means taking your time to do credit checks; perform criminal background checks, employment verification, and income verification (yes, separate from employment verification!); and—the most crucial one that landlords love to skip is reference—call *all* their references, including any former landlords they have listed. Talk to all of them for a minute or two, and listen for any subtle hints that the prospect might not be the upstanding citizen he or she claims to be. If your tenant has been involved in an eviction case in the past, this is a red flag. Having a high income is a great indicator of a reliable tenant, but if that high income comes hand in hand with a poor credit score and big debt, your tenant may not be willing or able to pay the rent on time (or at all).

Getting a few personal and professional references is a good idea to determine the kind of person your prospective tenant is. You have to be reasonable: if you kick out everyone who seems vaguely suspicious, you'll never get a tenant, but you also have to be canny and discerning. Any landlord who has performed the difficult search for the right tenant knows it's more cost effective to keep a tenant than to continually find new ones. Keeping a good tenant for a long time means less work, less stress, and reliable income. The goal of every landlord should be to attract and keep high-quality tenants, reducing turnover rates, and maximizing profit. The wrong tenants will turn your dream investment into a nightmare; the right ones will have you wondering what all the fuss over low-income neighborhoods is about in the first place.

Lesson Learned: *Every neighborhood has a broad range of people at all phases of life, and providing high-quality rental housing to attract the best people and doing your due diligence up front of vetting them will produce high rental income in any area; therefore, a low-income neighborhood does not mean low rent.*

Conclusion

I t can be intimidating to think about getting started in investing in real estate, but
as you can see from my story, I was able to
do it with little-to-no initial experience in the
area of real estate investment. So take these
lessons, and put them into practice, because
they really worked for me.

The hardest part is getting started, but
once you close on your first deal, it gets easier
going forward. Real estate investing can
be very expensive, but it can be done with
other people's money. Do not let your fear of
failure stop you from getting started. At any
given point in my journey, I could have gotten
discouraged, not started the process, or given
up along the way when faced with stumbling

blocks: lack of knowledge about real estate; useless foreclosure listings leading me all over the city and reaping nothing but frustration; finding out I didn't have enough for a down payment for a commercial property; losing all my money with the closing just weeks away; or realizing that managing a building was a daunting task and that hiring a manager for this particular project was too expensive. I did not let any of that stop me.

I faced many failures along the way, but it was through these failures that I learned some of my most valuable lessons. If you are thinking about generating some passive income for yourself and your family, let my story be of encouragement to you. I know you can do it. Because of my investments in real estate, I was able to retire from the corporate world before the age of forty. The key is getting started. So get off the fence, and just do it! Good luck!

ABOUT THE AUTHOR

Andrea Pryce was born into a large family of fourteen children in St. Catherine, Jamaica. She went on to graduate magna cum laude from York College, City University of New York, where she earned her bachelor's degree in accounting.

A certified public accountant, Pryce has more than fifteen years of leadership experience in the financial industry and is a former CEO of A&S Produce Corp., a retail company. She has also served on the board of directors for a number of charitable organizations and was a member of the New York City Volunteer Core for over four years.

Currently, Pryce is an adjunct professor at York College. In addition to investing in real estate, she conducts seminars throughout the United States, dedicated to helping individuals achieve financial freedom.

NOTES

INVESTMENT IDEAS